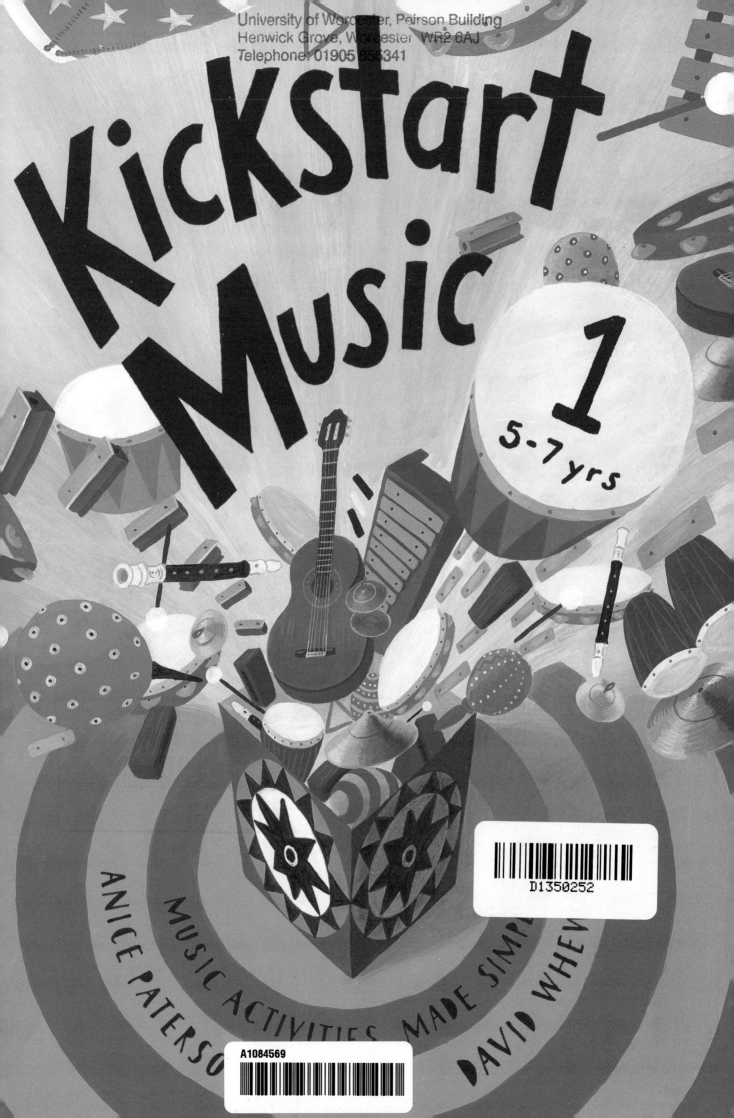

Kickstart Music

1

5-7 yrs

MUSIC ACTIVITIES MADE SIMPLE

ANICE PATERSON

DAVID WHEWAY

Contents

First published 2010

by A&C Black Publishers LTD

36 Soho Square, London, W1D 3QY

Copyright © Anice Paterson and David Wheway 2010

ISBN - 978 - 1 - 4081 - 23607

Edited by Laura White

Designed by Sara Oiestad, Jane Tetzlaff & Fi Grant

Cover illustration © David Dean

Inside illustrations © Peter Lubach

A&C Black uses paper produced with elemental chlorine-free pulp, harvested from managed sustainable forests.

Introducing Kickstart

The Kickstart Music series is written specifically with the generalist primary teacher in mind. Kickstart 1, 2 and 3 cover the whole of Key Stage 1 and 2, and Kickstart Music Early Years is for under-fives. The authors firmly believe that every practitioner can offer a positive musical experience to the children in his or her class.

DEVELOPMENT

The book broadly covers children's development from ages 5–7 (Key Stage One). However, it is hoped that many of these activities will be used again and again throughout their school life, possibly with increased challenge, and with slight changes in language use as the children get older.

STRUCTURE

The materials are divided into five sections. Listening, Rhythm, Movement, Pitch and Sounds and Invention are arranged broadly in progressive order within each section. However, progression in music is not always linear and it is perfectly acceptable for the activities to be used in a different order. Where it is essential to have completed certain other activities first, it will say so in the text. All the activities have been tried and tested successfully in the classroom.

Most activities are not just a single lesson plan. Some may last for ten minutes and serve as warm-up activities for others. Some may develop into projects lasting several weeks. Many activities will need re-visiting and further practice to achieve success. Remember that, in music, repeated practice is very important.

The current National Curriculum has acknowledged that all children within the primary phase of education have an entitlement to musical experiences.

The realisation of this entitlement depends on the confidence of the non-specialist teacher in music as it does in all other areas of the curriculum.

This book has therefore been prepared to support the generalist teacher by:

- Providing a development structure which is achievable.
- Providing outlines of activities which can be extended by teachers as they grow in confidence.
- Making the musical purpose clear and helping the teacher to understand the principles which underpin the musical activity.

Any school using all or most of the ideas will be giving its children a valuable musical experience. In the process, children will be provided with a sound foundation which will meet the requirements of music in the Curriculum.

Teachers in primary schools should endeavour to:
- Take opportunities to stimulate, sustain and enhance children's interest and awareness of sound.
- Provide a progressive, continuous and relevant musical experience.
- Continually assess and keep a record of each pupil's progress.
- Recognise individual need and facilitate additional support as and when required.
- Identify what music shares with other areas of the curriculum.
- Develop social skills and awareness through making music together.
- Develop an awareness of, and respect for, musical traditions in a variety of cultures and societies.

Music with your class

Here are some very simple pointers showing how to get the best out of the music activities with your class.

Children copy teachers

If you approach an activity in a positive, energetic and controlled way, the children will do the same.

Keep activities simple

Make sure that you know your materials well.

Children develop at different rates

In music, as in all other areas of the curriculum, keep an open mind about a child's musical potential. Children show it in a variety of ways.

Music is organised sound

It can happen anywhere – in the classroom, the playground, the hall, a music area. It can happen with a variety of sound sources – sounds in the environment, body sounds, sounds and rhythms from 'playing' junk as well as conventional instruments and voices.

Not all activities necessarily lead to a 'performed' product

Try to see performance as part of the process rather than just an end in itself. Encourage children to evaluate their own and other's individual and group performances through careful listening and discussion.

Encourage children to care for instruments.

If using instruments with a class, have them ready and close at hand at the start of the lesson to avoid losing time, and don't keep children waiting for too long before using them.

Children bring with them a wealth of musical experience

As well as previous school musical activities, the children may be developing additional skills outside the classroom at home, through instrumental learning or dance classes. Encourage them to be inventive and to value their own ideas and those of other children. Their parents, relations and other members of the local community may also share music with the class and school.

Develop clear ways of controlling noise

Use definite signals for stopping and starting, and demand immediate response. Give children the opportunity to lead an activity where appropriate. In some music activities, expect lots of noise – try to be tolerant of it. Encourage the tolerance of colleagues by explaining what you are doing and why.

Music helps those with special needs

Music provides opportunities for non-verbal self-expression, communication, motor control, co-ordination and social skills – all areas that are highly valued by the teacher of children with special needs. Many activities promote the opportunity for the development of social skills such as sharing, turn-taking, co-operating with others and appreciating the skills and ideas of other children in their group.

Whole curriculum planning

Activities in this book can support work in other areas of the curriculum. Other obvious inter-relationships may involve skills of a personal or social nature such as co-ordination, discrimination, decision-making, self-confidence, self-discipline, participation, co-operation, tolerance and cultural awareness.

Listening

This section includes activities which develop children's ability to listen carefully with concentration, identify and differentiate between sounds and textures, develop their musical memory and listen and respond to music.

Who's Next?

1. Give an instrument to one child, who plays it, while looking at another child.

2. The other child walks over to the child playing, takes the instrument and then returns to his/her place.

3. Repeat. Encourage the children playing the instruments to involve everyone in the group.

4. As the children progress, add extra instruments until three or more are being passed across the circle.

VARIANT

1. Select a child without an instrument who pretends to play one of the instruments held by another in the group. The group identifies the instrument he is pretending to play. Once they guess, the instrument is handed over to the child. Repeat.

2. A child with an instrument plays a steady pulse on his/her instrument. The rest of the group think of a song they know, to sing along to the pulse.

PURPOSE
To encourage turn-taking and begin to use instruments and soundmakers.

RESOURCES

A variety of unpitched percussion instruments and other soundmakers.

Ideas for songs

Slow pulse
'Hickory Dickory Dock'
'Incy Wincy Spider'
'Humpty Dumpty'

Fast pulse
'One man went to mow'
'Skip to my Lou'
'Pop goes the weasel'

How quiet can you be?

1. Children sit or stand in a circle, absolutely still.

2. The object/instrument (eg, jingle bells) is placed under a chair which stands in the centre of the circle.

3. One child sits blindfolded on the chair and must 'defend' the bells by listening for someone who tries to 'steal' them.

4. Teacher points to a child who silently tries to 'steal' the bells and escape.

5. Child 'defender' either puts her hand up or points in the direction of any sound. If caught out, the burglar resumes his place in the circle.

6. Repeat until the burglar is successful and takes the chair to defend the object for the next round. For younger/less experienced children, choose objects that are relatively easy to move quietly (eg, woodblocks).

EXTENSION

1. Place an object which makes a sound when moved under the chair. Can the 'defender' identify which object/instrument it is?

VARIANT

1. Play the 'Sleeping Tambourine' – not making any noise. Can all the children pass the tambourine carefully round the circle and not 'wake it up' (ie, not make a sound)? How many times did you wake it up? Can you do better next time?

PURPOSE

To encourage children to value stillness, and develop control and concentration in dealing with sound.

RESOURCES

A chair.

Any object/instrument selected by the children.

Making it last

1. Children sit or stand in a circle, raise their arms in the air and close their eyes.

2. Teacher plays a cymbal or chime bar (preferably a large, low one).

3. Children listen for the end of the sound. They lower their hands when they think it has finished.

4. How long did the sound last?

5. Repeat with other instruments and decide which one makes a sound that lasts the longest.

6. Several children around the circle have an instrument. Each plays in turn, but only when the sound of the previous person has completely stopped.

7. The rest of the class evaluate their performance, eg, did anyone come in too soon? Whose sound lasted the longest?

8. Repeat with the whole class.

EXTENSION

1. Try playing in different orders. Rather than around the circle, be the conductor and point to the child who should play next. Invite other children (without instruments) to be the conductor.

2. Record on paper the lengths of the children's sounds using symbols, for example:

for long ——————————
for short ——

Children should then play back what has been charted.

PURPOSE
To encourage concentration, stillness and the ability to listen acutely to quiet sounds.

RESOURCES
A variety of instruments and sound makers: cymbals, triangles, chime bars, woodblocks, sticks or saucepans.

REMEMBER
When playing with several children or the whole class, the children should hold their instruments in front of them waiting to play before the activity starts.

What can you hear?

1. Everyone sits, or preferably lies, on the floor with eyes closed.

2. Listen for a long time (perhaps a minute) to the sounds you hear.

3. Sit up and see how many noises everyone can remember.

4. They may hear:
   radiator humming,
   cars revving up,
   door shutting,
   chairs scraping on floor,
   child coughing.

5. Talk about sounds in groups:
   sounds from nature,
   man made sounds,
   human sounds,
   town or country sounds.

6. Find words to describe sounds:
   rough,
   loud,
   gentle,
   screeching.

7. Can you reproduce the sounds with your voices?

EXTENSION

1. Record some everyday sounds, for instance, lawn mower, stream, dogs barking. Find sound effects online or on a CD and play to the class. Can the children identify the sounds?

PURPOSE

To provide an opportunity for children to identify a variety of sounds and discuss their origin and quality.

RESOURCES

Recording device for the EXTENSION activity, or sound effects (CD or found online).

REMEMBER

This activity can be just as effective elsewhere, for example, outside on a nature walk, and can lead to some interesting learning about the activity which is generating each sound.

Can you remember?

1. Sit or stand in a circle with the instruments in the middle.

2. One child chooses a instrument/soundmaker, makes a sound and returns to his place.

3. The next child plays the same sound, then adds a new one of her own, possibly on a different instrument/soundmaker.

4. The next child plays the first two sounds, and adds a new one to the 'collection'.

5. Continue until it is no longer possible to remember the sequence accurately.

6. Continue this activity in small groups.

VARIANT

Play the activity with body sounds instead of instruments.

1. First child invents a body sound, eg, stamps foot.

2. Next child repeats the body sound and adds a new one.

3. Third child repeats second child's sound and invents a new one.

4. Each child makes only one new sound.

EXTENSION

1. Play the game as 'I went to market', but look for more accuracy in the way the sounds are copied,

   eg: "I went to market and bought a drum ('bang, bang, bang') cowbell ('ding, ding!'), a tambourine ('shake shake')."

PURPOSE
To develop musical memory and concentration.

RESOURCES

A large variety of sound sources, instruments and junk objects.

REMEMBER

Leave the instruments in the middle again after each child has played.

Hide and guess

1. The children choose lots of soundmakers/instruments to be put in a circle.

2. One child hides behind a screen.

3. Another child plays one of the sounds.

4. Can the hidden child guess which it was?

5. Keep the rest of the class involved by asking them to indicate whether the child guessed correctly, eg, thumbs up/thumbs down.

VARIANT

Have an identical group of instruments or soundmakers behind the screen to the ones in front. Child behind the screen plays one – a child in the class plays the correct one back.

EXTENSION

1. Four children go behind the screen. One speaks – who is it? Three speak together – who is left out? Recognising voices is a similar activity in terms of recognising sound quality.

2. The child behind the screen plays a sound pattern on an instrument (eg, 'bang bang, shake shake' on tambourine), which has to be copied by the child who identifies the instrument.

3. As (2), but child behind screen plays a sequence of soundmakers or instruments to copy – eg, tambourine, cowbells, drum, spoons, saucepan lid.

4. Three children behind screen play three instruments at once, then they play again, missing an instrument out – can the other children guess which instrument is missing?

PURPOSE
To refine the ability to distinguish between different sound qualities.

RESOURCES

A variety of instruments and soundmakers.

A screen or alternative.

REMEMBER

This activity can be carried out in a variety of ways, but must always involve careful listening, done slowly, quietly and thoughtfully.

Where is it?

1. One child leaves the room/the group.

2. Everyone else spreads out all over the room.

3. One child has an instrument and plays it quietly behind his back.

4. The child outside returns, moving among the group and listens carefully, trying to locate where the very quiet sound is coming from. Encourage all children to keep their backs turned from the seeking child.

5. When the sound is found, repeat the activity with another child.

6. Extend the activity by having two or three sounds to find and distinguish.

VARIANT

1. Blindfold a child in the centre of the circle and ask her to walk towards the sound source (instrument).

2. Teacher whispers the name of an animal into each child's ear – making sure there are two of each kind in the room. The children close their eyes and make their own animal noise while moving around the room. Can they find their 'partner', who will be making the same animal noise? When they find partners, they sit together to create a 'Noah's ark'.

PURPOSE

To develop the ability to listen to and locate very quiet sounds or those that are difficult to distinguish.

RESOURCES

A variety of instruments that ring, eg, bells or handchimes.

REMEMBER

Sounds made must be very quiet indeed.

Everyone has their hands behind their backs, pretending to have the instrument(s).

Listen and move

1. Play a pulse on the drum – children walk in time to the beat.

2. Change the speed of the pulse – all children walk in time at the new speed.

3. Play a pulse on the tambourine – children skip in time.

4. Change the speed of the pulse – children skip in the time at the new speed.

5. Repeat the process with a chime bar, to which children hop.

6. Change from drum to tambourine to chime bar – children must listen to 'musical' instruction and walk, hop or skip accordingly.

VARIANT

1. Try different rhythms on the same instrument:

   eg, regular pulse = ♩ ♩ ♩ ♩   walk = — — — — —

   skipping pulse = ♩ ♪ ♩ ♪   skip = — – — – —

   faster pulse = ♫♫♫♫   running = – – – – – –

   This needs more careful listening than the above.

2. The children make movements which 'feel' like the sounds, eg:
   • Shake your keys – everyone wiggles their fingers.
   • Ask a child to lead.
   • Use different sound sources and actions.

PURPOSE
To encourage careful and accurate responses in movement.

RESOURCES

A variety of instruments: drum, tambourine, chime bar, etc.

REMEMBER

Do not change either the sound or the speed of the pulse until every child is making an effort to move in time. Don't necessarily introduce the whole activity at the same session – gradual introduction may give better results.

Warm and cold/high and low

1. Ask a child to go out of the room or close eyes.

2. Hide a book (or anything agreed by the children).

3. The child comes in and has to find the hidden object.

4. As she or he gets nearer/warmer play the high note (G).
   As she or he gets further away/colder play the low note (C),
   eg:

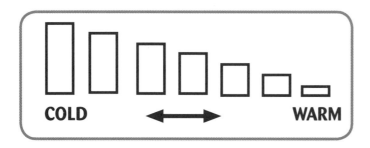

5. Involve the rest of the class by inviting them to point
   up for a high note and down for a low note.

PURPOSE
To encourage careful
and accurate response
to pitch.

RESOURCES

Something to hide, eg,
a book, a pencil.

A xylophone or a
variety of chime bars.

VARIANT

Grade the pitch levels used so that the children have more clues.
Therefore, the note gets higher as the child gets closer to the
object, and vice versa, eg:

EXTENSION

1. Narrow the pitch range so that it requires more precise listening
   discernment, (eg, **E - F,** see right).

Listening to Music

PURPOSE
To provide children with experience of and access to the widest possible range of music.

RESOURCES
Devices for playing music – computer, music centre, mp3 player.

Wide range of music – from the internet, on CD, from shops, from libraries, from the local music service.

Opportunities for hearing live music – other children, staff, parents and friends of the school, visiting artists.

1. Contexts in which listening to music might be effective at this age include:
   - To create a feeling of security by a familiar piece of a regular time of day.
   - To give an insight into an historical period or other culture.
   - To learn about artists and musicians of the present and the past.
   - To learn about instruments, voices and simple forms (eg, verse, chorus), and the ways in which composers have put music together.
   - For dancing or to create a theatrical effect.
   - To enhance the community feeling of the school.
   - To feel and spend time pleasurably.
   - To set a mood for working or calming down at different times of the day.

2. Listen for:
   - How music tells a story.
   - How music is used with words, movement, drama or film. What does it add?
   - How music describes an atmosphere or mood.
   - Particular instruments and sound qualities.
   - Ways of varying a tune.
   - Repetitions and patterns.

3. Music is useful as a trigger for creative writing, painting, dance and drama. The music needs to be heard several times and talked about before expecting anything more than a superficial response to a given piece.

   There are no right answers in this area. Children will respond in a variety of ways. Do not expect children to agree with your own emotional response to any music.

Discuss the instruments: Why you have chosen the piece of music? How does it makes you feel? Ask the children to comment and see if their views reflect yours.

4. Music is useful in understanding cultures and historical periods. Check over a year that children have been exposed to music in several styles and more than one cultural stream.

5. Ask the children about the sort of music they would like to hear more of. The internet now offers opportunities for children (possibly with support) to search for extracts.

REMEMBER

a) Initially use music familiar to you and music that you like. You will convey a sense of excitement much better that way.

b) Children will find it hard to concentrate for long periods unless they have a specific listening task. Active listening is always more likely to be more effective.

c) Relaxation and sheer enjoyment are also important. Comfortable surroundings help enormously.

d) Always make sure children know the name of the piece, its origin and, if known, its composer. They will develop the knowledge to find any piece they like and want to hear again, and they will develop more respect for those who compose and perform music.

e) Often children (and adults) find it difficult to express their feelings in words, which is why music is such a powerful medium. Try not to pressurise them to articulate feelings.

f) Use the internet to find music to listen to or video clips to make music for. Ask your local music library, local music service, and/or musical friends to suggest pieces for a specific purpose.

g) An entirely non-prescriptive list of recordings is provided on page 64, or visit the Kickstart Music pages on the www.acblack.com/music website, to help in the choice of music if needed.

h) Create a listening area in your classroom where children can select and play music. Headphones may be an optional extra, but be aware of the need to regulate the volume control.

Copycat

1. Children sit or stand in a circle with their instruments in front of them.

2. Teacher makes a rhythm using voice or body (eg, claps hands, hums) and 'passes' it to the child next to him.
   The child then copies the rhythm and plays it to the next child.

3. The rhythm travels from child to child round the circle.

4. Pass round rhythms – clapping, using rhythmic words or on an instrument.

eg:

    slow slow slow

or:

    slow quick quick slow

or:

    slow quick quick quick quick slow

PURPOSE

To refine listening skills by providing opportunities for children to repeat or reproduce what they have heard.

RESOURCES

A variety of instruments and soundmakers, one per child.

EXTENSION

1. Allow a child to lead the process.

2. Pass round a sequence of sounds, rather than just one, (eg, clap, click, slap, clap).

   eg, clap, click, slap, rest
       clap, slap slap, clap, click

   Allow a short space of time to elapse and then send the second 'message' or short sound round before the first one has gone around the circle. Listen to the result and discuss what has happened. Is this harder or easier to do? Does it sound interesting or messy?

Rhythm

This section includes activities which encourage children to develop a strong sense of pulse and rhythmic memory, to hear music in their heads, and to understand the use of repetitions to make music. Many will also help to develop their co-ordination and control of their bodies to help them play instruments.

Play and respond

1. Play a sound. One child copies it back. Play it again to the next child. Child copies again – and so on round at least part of the class, quickly.

2. Play a short rhythm. Child copies rhythm. Play a new rhythm and another child copies rhythm – and so on.

3. Repeat several times, encouraging the concept of turn-taking between yourself and the children.

4. Use the following phrases to help the children get the rhythm accurately:
   - 'I like Music'.
   - 'Do you like ice-cream?'
   - 'Where is my pet spider?'
   - 'Who is knocking at my door?'
   - 'We like bananas'.
   - 'Merrily, merrily, join in the dance'.

5. Play with about half the class for the first session. Promise that everyone will get a turn in the next few days.

PURPOSE
To encourage turn-taking and develop accurate response to rhythm.

RESOURCES
Drums, tabla, tambourine, bongos or tambour.

REMEMBER
Keep the rhythm very simple – 3 or 4 beats only.

Pass a rhythm parcel

1. Children sit or stand in a circle.

2. Decide on a rhythm, using words or rhythm word sounds, eg:

quick	quick	slow	slow	slow
John	- ny	stand	still	please
did	- dle	dum	dum	dum

3. Pass the rhythm round the circle, each person clapping, saying or singing it to 'la' after her neighbour.

4. Children make up new rhythms, words and sounds and think up other ways of passing them around, eg, on instruments or other soundmakers.

EXTENSION

1. Try passing the rhythm round in time to the pulse of some recorded music or the rhythm above. Pass the ball or bean bag round in time to the music as it is played or sung, ie. passing on every strong beat.

>   >
The Grand old Duke of York

2. When the response is accurate, try passing the ball and a rhythm round in time to the pulse, to a variety of rhymes/songs.

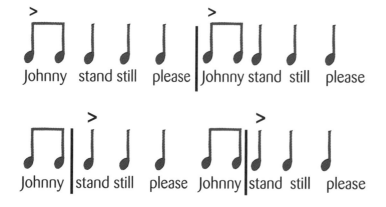

PURPOSE
To develop response to pulse and accurate recall of rhythmic patterns.

RESOURCES

For the Extension: a piece of recorded music or a well known song with strong, clear beats, eg, 'Chatanooga Choo Choo', 'The Grand Old Duke of York'.

Ball or bean bag.

REMEMBER

Accuracy in rhythm and pulse takes a long time (and much practice) to achieve. Expect to do this activity many times to acquire the skills.

Traffic lights

1. Sing/speak a song or rhyme the children know well, eg:
   * 'Three blind mice'.
   * 'There was an old woman'.
   * 'Head and Shoulders baby'.
   * 'Pizza hut song'.

2. When you show the green light to the children they sing/speak the rhyme.

3. When you show the red light to the children they continue to 'sing'/think it inside their heads or sing it very quietly.

4. Show the green light again. Everybody sings aloud from where they have got to. Did they all get to the same point of the song in their heads as the same time? If not, why not?

5. Ask a child to operate the lights.

EXTENSION:

1. Work with songs with varying pulses (or beats), eg:
   * 'My bonnie lies over the ocean'.
   * 'Row, row, row your boat'.
   * 'She'll be coming round the mountain'.
   * 'Michael Finnigan'.

PURPOSE

To develop children's inner sense of pulse and the ability to hear in their heads.

RESOURCES

Two sets of traffic lights (see illustration). Colour in the green light on one, red on the other.

REMEMBER

Change the lights at the beginnings and ends of phrases more often as the children become proficient.

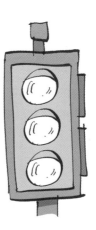

Messages

1. Children sit or stand in a circle.

2. Teacher calls out an instruction at the same time as tapping out its rhythm on the claves, eg:

    Stand up!

    The children respond with the appropriate action.

3. Teacher taps and calls out another instruction, eg:

    Sit down now!

    The children respond.

4. Teacher taps and calls out another instruction, eg:

    Wig-gle your fin - gers!

    The children respond.

5. Teacher stops calling out the words so that the children listen and respond only to the 'messages' (rhythms) on the claves.

EXTENSION

1. Gradually refine the activity a little each session by using more complex instructions and/or rhythms.

PURPOSE

To develop musical memory and sense of rhythm through listening to and discriminating between long and short sounds.

RESOURCES

Rhythm sticks, claves or a beater on a table.

REMEMBER

The rhythms must be very strong and clear. Make sure you have the rhythms right by saying the words many times to yourself, eg: "Sit down now/Sit down now/Sit down now."

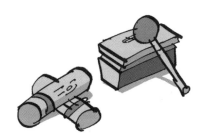

Lollipops

1. Chant the following rhyme very rhythmically.

> Lollipop, lollipop   lick, lick, lick
> Lollipop, lollipop   click, click, click
> Lollipop, lollipop   slap, slap, slap
> Lollipop, lollipop   clap, clap, clap

2. Chant the rhyme again, with the appropriate actions.
(pretend to lick for "lick, lick, lick").

3. Chant it while marching around to a pulse given by a drum or
pitched instrument.

4. Divide the children into two groups. Group A chants the rhyme
while group B does the actions, and vice versa.

EXTENSION

1. Add a third group, who play instruments or soundmakers,
such as claves, sticks, or screw top plastic bottles filled with
sugar, lentils or pulses, during the actions.

2. One group of children chants "lollipop" very quietly and
continuously throughout the rhyme.

3. Try in four groups, as a round.

Group 1 chants "lollipop", continuously enjoying the "Pop"
sound, to make a rhythmic 'backing'.
Group 2 starts its chant and says it all the way through.
Group 3 starts it after the first line when Group 2 finishes
"Lollipop, lollipop", and so on.
To end, all join Group 1 and say
"Lollipop, lollipop, POP! POP! POP!"

PURPOSE
To develop children's
physical response to
rhythmic pulse.

RESOURCES
A variety of
instruments.

Wibble wobble

1. Use skipping rhymes or playground chants such as Jelly on a plate.

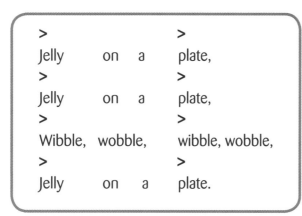

> >
Jelly   on a   plate,
> >
Jelly   on a   plate,
> >
Wibble, wobble,   wibble, wobble,
> >
Jelly   on a   plate.

PURPOSE
To develop children's physical co-ordination using the rhythm of a rhyme.

RESOURCES
A variety of instruments for the progression.

2. Children clap hands in time to the pulse. (>)

3. Each child finds a partner and claps alternate claps with partner's hands.

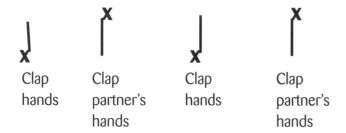

Clap
hands

Clap
partner's
hands

Clap
hands

Clap
partner's
hands

4. Pairs of children work out a clapping pattern together to accompany the rhyme.

5. Teach it to the rest of the class.

EXTENSION

1. Use instruments instead of clapping, so that pairs of children can work out patterns using contrasting instruments.
Try this with other songs/rhymes such as 'Each peach pear plum' or 'One potato, two potato'.

Name that tune

1. Choose two songs the children know well, for example:
   - 'Daddy's taking us to the zoo tomorrow.'
   - 'The wheels on the bus.'
   - 'Daisy Daisy.'

2. Sing them through together.

3. Clap the rhythm of the songs together. It might be easier to introduce the rhythm in small sections.

4. Play the rhythms on an instrument.

5. Clap one of the rhythms, and ask the children to identify which song it is.

6. Clap or play an extract of one of them – perhaps the opening or the beginning of the chorus. Can the children work out which song it is from?

7. Make the extract more difficult – try using the second or last line.

8. Increase the range of songs.

VARIANT

1. As a class, make up chants using names, cars, villages, sporting teams, things to eat, etc. Agree the rhythm together, eg:

   Sean, James, Jayesh, John,
   Sarah, Jean, Kirti, Yvonne.

   Play the rhythm of one of your chants. Can the children identify the groups of names you are playing?

PURPOSE
To develop children's rhythmic memory.

RESOURCES

A variety of instruments.

A variety of songs (see pg, 64 or the Kickstart Music section of www. acblack.com).

Clapping

1. Everyone sits or stands in a circle.

2. Teacher claps hands for 3 beats and then rests for 3 beats:

rest   rest   rest

3. Try a silent movement for the 3 rests, eg, shake fist 3 times (below).

shake shake shake
fist   fist   fist

4. Repeat this a few times without pausing between claps and rests.

5. When the rhythm is set up well, keep going. In the rests, say your name, and then a few more to demonstrate:

> Clap clap clap – Mi-ster Jones
> Clap clap clap – Samuel Postle-thwaite
> Clap clap clap – Ja-son Morley

6. Go round the circle with each child saying their name:
3 claps / Jenny Parkinson / 3 claps / Dipak Patel/
3 claps/Christopher Jones/3 claps/Anne Sharp/3 claps

Keep in time, however long or short the name is.

EXTENSION

1. Use other ideas for the gap, for example, favourite food, TV programmes, what makes you happy or sad.

PURPOSE
To develop a strengthened sense of rhythm and pulse.

REMEMBER

Keeping a regular pulse is much more important than getting a word right, so if a child stumbles, keep going.

Rhythm and clocks

1. Children chant steadily, like a wristwatch:
   "ticka tocka ticka tocka".

2. Children change the chant to imitate a grandfather clock, using
   a bigger, louder, rounder sound:
   "Tick Tock Tick Tock".

3. Change to Big Ben chant, with a big, loud, longer sound:
   "BOING!   BOING!"

4. Split into three groups, each chanting one of the clock sounds
   that the children have practised. The teacher keeps a steady,
   light pulse on a drum. Each group keeps its clock sound going.

5. Try bringing each sound in and out, one after the other, and
   build to a climax. When the children are comfortable with the
   chant, allow individual children to act as conductors too.

ticka tocka	ticka tocka	ticka tocka	ticka tocka
Tick	Tock	Tick	Tock
BOING!		BOING!	

PURPOSE

To reinforce children's
sense of keeping in
time and to introduce
the skill of writing
rhythm down.

RESOURCES

Pictures of any
sorts of clocks – Big
Ben, Grandfather,
stopwatch (below).

Paper, card and
pencils.

EXTENSION

1. Devise symbols on cards:

   ticka tocka   Tick Tock   BOING!

   Hold them up for groups to 'play' in turn.

2. Divide the class into a singing and an accompaniment group.
   The accompaniment group maintains some/all of the ideas
   above – to which the singing group sings: 'My Grandfather's
   Clock'.

Shake it all about

PURPOSE
To develop strong rhythmic control and understanding.

RESOURCES
Keyboard rhythm box, rhythm programmes such as ESP Rhythm Maker, and/or recordings of music with a very strong beat. See pg. 64 or the Kickstart Music section of www. acblack.com for suggestions.

All children find a space. Put on music loud enough for everyone to hear. Teacher leads a rhythmic dance session in one or more of the following ways:

1. Start with a piece with a regular count of four – a rock beat or a march.

    Teacher: "Give me a **one**, a **two**, a **one** two three four."
    Children: "a **one**, a **two**, a **one** two three four."

    Do these actions in time with the music, the children following the teacher. Repeat lots of times.

    Shake, shake, shake, shake,
    (shaking right fist followed by left fist)
    Wave, wave, wave, wave,
    (waving right hand followed by left hand)
    Bob, bob, bob, bob,
    (bob down and up again in time)
    Wiggle, wiggle, wiggle, wiggle,
    (wiggling)
    Stamp, stamp, stamp, stamp,
    (stamping)
    Shuffle, shuffle, shuffle, shuffle.
    (shuffling or sliding around the floor)

    The most important thing is to encourage children to stay exactly in time with the music, feeling the pulse in their body. Keep doing it until virtually everyone is moving at exactly the same time. With very young children this may take some time.

2. Change to music with a count of three – a waltz or an 'oom cha cha' rhythm (eg, 'Oom pah pah' from 'Oliver!').

    Teacher: "Give me a **one** two three, **one** two three."
    Children: "**one** two three, **one** two three."

Everyone says the words while doing the actions:

"Oom cha cha, Oom cha cha, Oom cha cha, Oom cha cha,"
(lean to one side, and the other)

"Boom ching ching, Boom ching ching, Boom ching ching,"
(stamp, hand shake, hand shake)

"Wow, yes, yes, Wow, yes, yes, Wow, yes, yes,"
(arms up and down in time)

And so on – make up your own words and movements to fit the music.

3. Put on a new piece of music and ask the children to work out physically how many beats there are – probably two, three or four. Divide the children into pairs and start the music again. Leave it on for some time while the children get the feel of it.

4. Give the children time to work out a rhythmic routine in pairs (using movement or sounds). Then join the pairs together and get each pair to teach the others their 'routine'.

5. Demonstrate finished routines to the rest of the class.

EXTENSION

1. Give six children a selection of percussion instruments/ soundmakers to play gently with the rhythms, or emphasise the key words ("wow", "boom", etc) while the others move. Give them time to work and practise.

> **REMEMBER**
>
> It is very important that the children can feel the beat they are moving on quite strongly before they spend time devising routines themselves. Some will take much longer to find the beat than others.
>
> This activity is ideal for a short time at any time of the day when there is a need to change children's focus from one activity to another.
>
> Each different piece of music used makes it feel like a different activity every time.

Talking drums

1. Children sit in a circle.

2. Teacher sits in the middle of the circle with a drum.

3. One child sits opposite with a drum of her own.

4. 'Talk' with the drums – the teacher plays a rhythm as if it were a musical question. A child plays back with a rhythm that could be a musical answer. At first, you can speak as you play, eg:

Teacher   Child (A)

♩ ♩ ♩   ♩ ♩♫ ♩

Rhythm sounds like: (How are you?) (I'm ve - ry well.)

5. When everyone understands the principle, the teacher changes with a child B and child A asks the next 'question'.

6. It's fine to use words to start with, but after a while encourage children to ask musical 'questions' without any words and to answer without words too.

EXTENSION

1. Use different unpitched instruments for the question and the answer, eg, drum answered by bells.

2. Play the questions loud or soft/fast or slow. Does the answer have to be the same?

3. Use two pitched instruments for the question and answer. Does it make a sort of tune?

PURPOSE
To encourage children to experiment with rhythm using instruments as the medium.

RESOURCES

A tabla or other drum.

A variety of other instruments.

REMEMBER

If the children find this hard, try whispering the words of the question or answer rhythms to start with. Aim to be able to do it without words, just with rhythms.

Movement

This section includes activities which will help children to move freely and rhythmically to music, develop strong co-ordination for the playing of instruments and explore their feeling responses to music.

Stretch and dance

1. Children stand in a circle with space around them. All follow the teacher's lead.

2. Stretch up as high as possible with your hands, higher and higher, fingers to the ceiling. Drop as low as possible and touch the floor. Repeat lots of times – and relax.

3. Stretch your arms out as far as you can in front of you, then above your head, open them up and return to by your sides. Repeat many times – and relax.

4. Hands by sides, move your right arm down your right side as far as possible and return to upright. Repeat with left arm – and relax.

5. Move head slowly from side to side and drop down to your neck – and relax.

6. Move your face in every possible way; grimace, like a fish, open mouth wide in a yawn – and relax.

7. Wave your arms from side to side, shake your wrists and wriggle your fingers while you do so.

8. Bend down to touch your toes and then slowly uncurl to upright, and then stretch as far up as you can. Slowly curl up again and down to the first position.

PURPOSE

To warm up the body before movement and music activities.

REMEMBER

Warming up the body is very important before any physical exercise. Invent any simple exercise that seems appropriate. Warming up the voice is just as important – the vocal cords are muscles as well. (See 'Find your voice', page 41).

Conducting

1. Each child has an instrument/soundmaker.

2. Devise simple instructions for the group to follow, eg: hands by side = don't play; hands in the air = play.

3. Ask the children to form a circle. The conductor (teacher or child) stands in the middle of the circle and tells all children to play their instrument using the simple hand signals above.

VARIANT

1. Try different hand positions for different volumes (eg, raising them to get louder). Can the children gradually get louder ('crescendo') and quieter ('diminuendo')?

2. Point to specific children to start or stop playing, using appropriate signals for start and stop.

PURPOSE

To encourage children to make decisions, and develop the ability to stop and start when playing an instrument.

RESOURCES

A variety of instruments and/or soundmakers.

REMEMBER

This activity is very good for encouraging shy children to become involved in activities.

With children with special needs who make involuntary movements, try playing to their movements. This can be very rewarding for the child but usually requires helpers to play the instruments at the precise moment the child moves.

Wakey wakey!

1. Talk with the children about the things we might do when we get up in the morning:
   - Jump out of bed.
   - Yawn and stretch.
   - Have a bath.
   - Eat our toast.
   - Brush our hair.
   - Clean our teeth.
   - Walk to school.

2. Choose a child to tell the story of what he did this morning.

3. When the child mentions a suitable activity, sing, to the tune of 'Here we go round the Mulberry Bush', the appropriate words to the activity. The children can join in at any point, eg:

   This is the way we jump out of bed,
   Jump out of bed, jump out of bed,
   This is the way we jump out of bed,
   When we get up in the morning.

   Try to make the children actually jump when they say "jump", as it reinforces the stress in the music. Make up actions for other verses too – eg, pretend to brush your hair or clean your teeth.

PURPOSE
To develop the early stages of responsive movement in children.

RESOURCES

The tune of 'Here we go round the Mulberry Bush'.

Grandfather, father and son

1. Children find a space.

2. Teacher plays a drum beat slowly – children walk slowly around the room, like a grandad.

   Teacher says the rhyme as the children move in time:

   > Slowly, slowly,
   > Walks my grandad,
   > Leaning hard upon his stick.
   > Wait for me, lad, says my grandad,
   > **I'm too old, I can't be quick**.

3. Speed up the drum beat – ask the children, "who's walking now?"

   Say this rhyme as the children move along faster:

   > My dad goes off to work each day,
   > He's brisk – and can't be late,
   > But when he comes home later on
   > **It's at a slower rate.**

   (Substitute 'Mum' and 'she' here if the children want.)

4. Speed up the drum beat – "who's walking now?"
   Say this rhyme as the children move even faster:

   > When I go off to meet my friends
   > My walk gets faster – faster,
   > Until both feet are off the ground
   > **As I run faster – faster.**

VARIANT

1. Use other instruments to vary the sounds for grandad, father and son.

2. Encourage the children to join in with the last line (in bold) of each verse when confident.

PURPOSE

To encourage children to feel mood and speed and convey it through movement.

RESOURCES

A drum.
The rhyme (see main activity text) for the teacher to say – better if it's known by heart.

The frightened tortoise

1. Children find a space.

2. Talk with the children about tortoises and what they do when they are frightened.

3. Bang the drum very loudly – all the children curl up and hide their heads 'in their shells'.

4. Begin playing the drum very quietly. As the quiet sound continues, the 'tortoises' become more confident and gradually uncurl and extend their limbs, feeling the space around them.

5. Bang the drum very loudly again – they withdraw again quickly back into their shells. Repeat the activity.

VARIANT

1. Think of other animals' defences and do the equivalent actions, eg:
   - Hedgehogs – curling into a ball and rolling away.
   - Zebras – fleeing at great speed from a lion.
   - Bird – flying away from a cat pouncing.

2. Get gradually louder or faster with the drum to indicate the animal getting nearer, and conversely quieter and slower to indicate the danger receding.

3. A child can lead this activity when it is well known.

PURPOSE
To provide an opportunity to combine sound, movement and feeling.

RESOURCES
A drum.

Ribbons

1. Children find a space, holding their ribbons.

2. Without music, everyone experiments to see what shapes they can make in the air with the ribbons – using just hands, whole arms, and whole body.

3. Put on the first musical excerpt. Listen for a short time while everyone thinks through the movements he or she wants to make.

4. Put the music on again. Everyone moves his or her ribbon freely in the air in response to the mood of the music.

VARIANT

1. A few agreed movements could be 'choreographed' by the whole class.

2. Children in groups of four. Two hold the ribbons between them and move them up and down like waves The other two work on a 'routine' to the music which involves them crossing, swimming through, below and around the ribbons.

3. Use a large sheet (the ideal is a huge piece of coloured material). Four children hold the corners and, to some gentle music, the other children weave under, round and over it as the four lift it and lower it – all in the gentle mood of the music.

PURPOSE
To encourage free movement to music.

RESOURCES

Music – a selection of short, varied, contrasting excerpts.

A piece of ribbon or a long strip of paper (about a metre long) for each child.

Hokey cokey

1. Make a large circle, holding hands.

2. Spend some time checking that the children know their left sides (arm, leg, etc) from their right sides.

3. Sing the 'Hokey Cokey' song, quite slowly.

   You put your left arm in, your left arm out,
   In, out, in, out, and shake it all about.
   You do the Hokey Cokey and you turn around,
   That's what it's all about ...

4. Put in (and out) legs, head, whole body.

   At this stage, sing the song slowly. At the beginning of each new action, check that all the children are using the same limb.

A camel's hump

1. Everyone learns the rhyme:

   I'd like to go over the desert,
   Bumpety, bumpety, bump. (*)
   Riding on top of a camel's
   Humpity, humpity, hump. (*)

2. Children spread out and stand in a space.

3. Bend the knees on the pulse (or beat).

4. Clap at the end of the 2nd and 4th lines (*).

5. Try it moving around the room, or in a line.

VARIANT

1. Write another verse – for example:

   I'd like to go down to the river,
   Paddle, a swash and a swish,
   Riding my wobbly kayak,
   Swish and a swash and a fish!

   (Actions: paddling and falling over at the end.)

2. Two children devise a rhythmic accompaniment with pitched
   or unpitched percussion and perform with the group. Take
   it in turns for children to accompany everyone saying the
   rhymes.

PURPOSE
To develop a physical
response to a strict,
measured pulse (or
beat).

RESOURCES

A large picture of a
camel (optional).

Hands together

Try any of these co-ordination games.

1. Handclapping with a partner:
   - Hands together then left hand to partner.
   - Hands together then right hand to partner.
   - Hands together then both hands to partner.

2. Tap your head rhythmically with one hand.
   Now try rubbing your tummy round and round with
   the other hand. When you are good at it, change hands over.

3. Hold right ear with left hand and nose with right hand.
   Then swap sides. Try it getting faster!

EXTENSION

Other activities that build co-ordination skills might include:

1. Marching in time and clapping on every **other** beat.

1   **2**   **3**   **4**

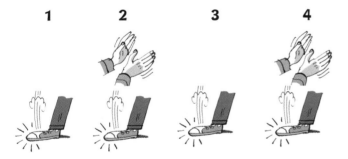

2. Sing songs with actions, for example:
   - 'Dingle Dangle Scarecrow.'
   - 'Long Legged Sailor.'
   - 'Tall Straw Hat.'
   - 'One, two, three, Open your eyes and see.'
   - 'Five Little Speckled frogs.'

PURPOSE
To build the physical co-ordination necessary for the development of instrumental skills.

REMEMBER

Any exercise which improves children's co-ordination will help when they need to play instruments on the beat – so any familiar action songs, like 'One potato, two potato', done rhythmically, also work very well.

Music, Movement and Mood

PURPOSE

To encourage children to move expressively to music.

1. Children lie flat on the floor in a large space.

2. Listen to a very short extract from 'La Mer', with eyes closed.

3. Sit up. Talk with the children about movements for:
   - Drops of water.
   - Smooth/calm sea.
   - Waves.
   - High/low movements of the waves.
   - Any other ideas supplied by the children.

4. Children lie on the floor again. As the music starts, they move in the way they feel is right for themselves.

EXTENSION

1. Sit up. Use a more lively piece – the children begin to move their arms and hands only to express the movement as they hear it. Give them encouragement to use all the space around them, and reflect the mood of the music they hear.

2. Stand up. In pairs, children develop some steps or movements to go with the piece of music. Practise doing so in time with each other.

This activity can be done in conjunction with 'Ribbons' page 34 and 'Soundscape page 61).

3. Change pairs. Play the music again and each child teaches the new partner to do 'their' movements. Make sure the mood of the movements matches the music, eg, if the music is 'jaunty', their steps should be 'jaunty'. Similarly, if the music is still, the movements will be very slow and simple.

4. Use large pieces of material to develop dance movements in pairs, reflecting the feeling of the music or their imaginative exploration of it.

REMEMBER

Feeling the expressiveness in music cannot be forced. It can be done with a whole range of relatively quiet music of the teacher's choice, and the children can say what it makes them think of. There are no right or wrong answers in relation to feeling and music.

The children will not all move in the same way. Do not insist on uniformity – just make sure the ideas have been discussed thoroughly. It also helps to hear the music several times. Make sure they know what the music is and who wrote it.

This activity works particularly well with children with special needs.

Pulse walk

1. Children spread out, so that nobody is touching anyone else.

2. Beat out a pulse on a drum – the children walk on the pulse.

3. Start counting 1, 2, 3, 4 on the pulse – the children count out loud as they walk.

4. Introduce a clap instead of a step on beat number 1. The children change direction on the clap, eg:

1 2 3 4	clap 2 3 4	clap 2 3 4
	(change)	(change)

5. Replace the clap with a tambourine.

VARIANT

1. Try the same exercise with different numbers of beats, eg, 3, 5, 6, 7 etc – before changing direction.

2. Play the tambourine for a change of direction on more unpredictable beats, eg:

1   2   🪘   4 | 1   2   🪘   4 |

OR

1   2   🪘   4 | 1   🪘   3   4 |

PURPOSE
To develop a physical response to a strict, measured pulse (or beat).

RESOURCES

A tambourine.
A drum.

Pitch

This section includes activities which will help children to find their voice, sing with enjoyment and musicality, improve their pitch discrimination and begin to improvise music. Some activities will also help children to understand the role of simple notations to record music.

Find your voice

Try any or all of the following for no more than five minutes at the beginning of any session using the voice. The children stand up during each activity.

1. Explosions – find all the consonants which make an explosive sound, eg, "pppp", "bbbb", "gggg", "tttt", "dddd". Say them lots of times slowly and then get faster and/or as explosive as possible.

2. Make sounds like a siren – demonstrate from as low as you can to as high as you can, then ask the children to do the same – on vowels such as "aah", "eee" and "ooh". Be a rocket too, on "whoosh!"

3. Hum any note quietly – count 4, then eight, on each breath and see if the children can hold it that long. Then hum the note loudly and see if they can hold it for as long as they held the quiet note.

4. Sing "meow" on one note mouthing the word in an exaggerated fashion very slowly. Make sure the children's mouths really move around a lot. Sing it on different notes (higher or lower), and listen to whether the children are singing accurately. When you are confident they can control their pitch, sing it step by step up a scale, still very slowly, in order to give every child a chance to pick up the pitch accurately.

PURPOSE
To warm up the voice for singing.

REMEMBER

Some children will take longer to find their voice accurately than others. Allow them enough time. It may take years but they must keep practising.

High and low

1. Play two notes, one low and one high.

2. Children stand for the high notes and sit for the low. Do this many times using different notes.

3. All children have access to an instrument. Everyone decides which instruments play high or low sounds or both. This time the teacher stretches high and the children with high instruments play. The teacher crouches low and the children with low instruments play – and so on.

4. Give children the chance to lead.

EXTENSION

1. Increase the numbers of different notes/pitches played. Check again that everyone agrees which order they should be played in – high to low or vice versa.

2. Introduce further movement levels for of the extra pitches, eg:
   - Play a low note – crouch as low as possible.
   - Play a bit higher – sitting or knees bend.
   - Play a bit higher – standing but shoulders drooping.
   - Play a very high note – on tip toe with arms stretched.

PURPOSE

To encourage the identification of high and low sounds.

RESOURCES

Stand a xylophone or glockenspiel on end with high (smaller) notes at the top, so children can make a physical association between high and low.

REMEMBER

Moving up and down with the body can be progressively refined to an impressive degree. If the gap between the notes is very large, children crouch low and stretch high. If the gap is very small they need hardly move at all.

All around the house

1. Discuss the pictures with the children. Be sure they know what they are and whether the objects normally live upstairs or downstairs. Remember, some children may live in bungalows or flats.

2. Children sit in a circle with the house and the pictures of the furniture in the middle.

3. Play two notes: a high one for the 'upstairs' note, and a low one for the 'downstairs' note.

4. Walk around the circle playing the two notes alternately or as a tune. If possible, do so without the children being able to see what you are playing.

5. Stand behind a child and stop playing. The child has to decide whether you stopped on an upstairs note or a downstairs note, and find an appropriate picture to put in the house.

6. Continue until all furniture has been allocated.

7. Make it progressively harder by lowering the high note so that the two notes are much closer together.

8. Allow a child to play upstairs and downstairs notes.

9. Try the same activity, but sing the two notes instead of playing them. You can then be sure that the children are hearing it rather than peeking a look at the instrument.

PURPOSE

To encourage the development of pitch discrimination.

RESOURCES

A large diagram of the inside of a house.

Pictures of objects found in a house, eg, bath, cooker.

Alternatively, use a toy house with loose furniture.

Two notes – such as a high and low chime bar or hand chimes for ease of movement, or xylophone if chimes aren't available.

REMEMBER

This can work well in a music area with pairs of children working together. Be sure to use this outline over several sessions or weeks to develop the aural skill.

Mountaineering

Copy/photocopy and enlarge the diagrams below
and position them so that the children can see them.
This activity is best done after High and low, page 42.

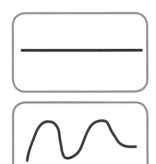
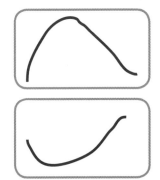

1. Children face the display.

2. The teacher 'walks' the mountaineer/pointer up and down the
   mountains, using their voice to mirror the shapes.

3. Children make their voices do the same, up and down, high
   and low, using any vocal sound.

4. Children draw shapes in the air in response to the
   teacher's voice rising and falling.

5. Children draw the shapes they hear on paper.

6. Children draw their own shapes for others in the class to 'read'.

EXTENSION

1. Allow groups of children to use the cards independently to
   find the shapes on instruments in a music area.

PURPOSE

To encourage
awareness of high
and low sounds using
the voice and relate
the sounds to simple
written symbols.

RESOURCES

Workcards prepared
with landscape
shapes.

Felt pens, pencils.

Pointer (with
mountaineer
attached).

More mountain
shapes on display.

REMEMBER

Not all children will find
their voices immediately
or be able to control
them well straight away.

Find the note!

1. Teacher and children sit in a circle.

2. A child is asked to think of a note, hum it and hold on to it whilst everyone tries to hum the same note.

3. The same child makes a signal when he wants everyone to stop and listen to the new note he is humming.

4. Everyone tries to hum the new note.

5. Repeat three or four times before giving another child a chance to lead.

EXTENSION

1. A child is asked to hum or sing two or three different notes (eg, middle range note, high note, low note) slowly. If necessary, copy or repeat it back to the class. How many children can show with their hands in the air the path of the notes as they are hummed?

2. Repeat activity above. While it is going on, can anyone draw on the board the path of the notes as they move from one to another?

3. Can the children read the same drawing back? A child points along the shape of the path on the board and one or all of the children hum it.

PURPOSE
To encourage awareness of pitch and observation of 'stop' and 'start' signals, and to give children a chance to lead.

REMEMBER

Not every child will be able to hum the given note immediately. Children's voices develop at different rates.

Make sure the signal to stop is well rehearsed.

Here I come!

1. Play G and E on chime bars until everyone knows the sounds well.

G   E

2. Teacher sings: Children sing:

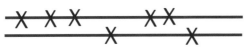

G ──×──   ──×──
E ×──×──   ──×──

Here I come!   Where from?

G ×────   ──×─×─×──
E ──×──   ────×──

Leicester!   What's in your jug?

G ×─×────   ─×─×─×──×─×──
E ────×──   ────×────×──

Orange juice!   Pour me some please in my mug.

3. When the children have sung "Pour me some please …", the teacher goes to one child in the circle and pours her a glass of orange juice (probably pretend).

4. That child then begins the song again instead of the teacher. This time, substitute another drink. No drink may be repeated.

VARIANT

1. Make up other rhymes and actions – here are some ideas for the last three lines:

   What's in your bag?   What's your name?
   My pencils   Daniel
   Can I have some for my bag?   Daniel is a funny/super name!

2. Pick two other notes to sing with – eg, A and E or C and G.

PURPOSE

To encourage children to have a musical conversation – question and answer.

RESOURCES

Glockenspiel or chime bars – notes E and G

REMEMBER

Follow natural speech rhythms – make sure the rhythm of the song is exactly as you would say it in normal speech.

Try not to allow any gaps between teacher and children singing; between question and answer.

Make your own tune

1. Children work in pairs or on their own in a 'music area', with the instrument(s) between them.

2. Children invent simple melodies that will go with the rhymes, using only the two notes provided and .

3. Practise tunes thoroughly.

4. Encourage any children who wish to play their creations to the rest of the class to do so.

5. The class can accompany quietly by patting their knees at a steady pulse. Make sure this accompaniment is sensitive and non-threatening to the child playing the tune.

EXTENSION

1. Extend the number of notes used to three notes:

| E | | G | | A |

2. When children have a well-practised tune they have played to the class, give some other children a simple rhythm accompaniment to go with it, eg:
   - Bells to play on the beat.
   - A tambourine roll at the end.
   - A quiet clap all the way through as a regular beat.

PURPOSE
To encourage children to develop basic improvisational skills.

RESOURCES

Chime bars E and G plus A for Extension, or glockenspiel/ xylophone with the rest of the notes removed.

Rhymes the children know well (any rhyme will do, but if you can't think of one, why not start with 'Incy Wincy Spider'?)

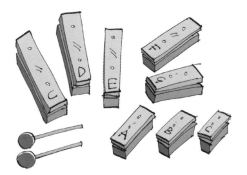

Gone fishing

1. Children sit in a circle.

2. The teacher plays the notes $\boxed{E}$ and $\boxed{G}$ many times until the children are familiar with them. The children play the notes too (on chime bars or xylophones).

3. Say the words below in the natural rhythm of speech.

4. Sing the words in a natural speech rhythm using any of the two notes in any order. An example below is,

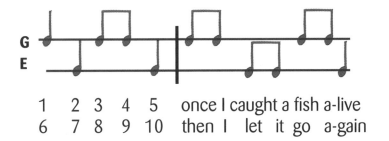

```
G
E
    1   2  3  4   5    once I caught a fish a-live
    6   7  8  9  10    then I  let it  go a-gain
```

5. Sing the song as a game. Pass the ball round the circle while the song is sung. The child holding the ball at the end must sing the song with the name of another animal or fish. Repeat many times.

VARIANT

1. Leave the chime bars for the children to work out the tune independently or in groups.

2. Try the same two notes with other words or action songs, eg:
   Touch your shoulders, touch your knees,
   Raise your arms and drop them, please!
   Touch your ankles, touch your toes,
   Pull your ears and touch your nose!

PURPOSE
To encourage children to sing on two notes of definite pitch.

RESOURCES

Chime bars or glockenspiel, notes $\boxed{E}$ and $\boxed{G}$

A ball.

Follow my leader

1. Using natural speech rhythm (therefore, how you would naturally say the words) and the notes E and G, the leader sings through the song below.
Everyone repeats the song as many times as necessary until everyone is comfortable with the two notes.

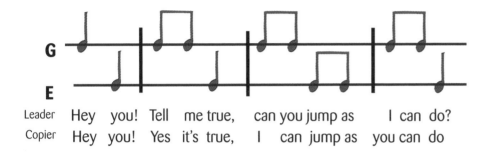

Leader Hey you! Tell me true, can you jump as I can do?
Copier Hey you! Yes it's true, I can jump as you can do

2. The leader sings the song through again, but this time chooses a different action word (eg, wave, sleep, write).
Everyone repeats.

3. The leader makes up a different action each time and the children repeat, copying the actions.

4. Children take turns at being the leader.

PURPOSE
To listen to and sing two notes accurately and give children the opportunity to lead.

RESOURCES
Chime bars, xylophone or glockenspiel, notes E and G

REMEMBER
Use the natural rhythms of speech to start with.

Pay attention to accuracy in pitching the two notes.

Use the chime bars to help and to accompany the singing.

Singing with young children

PURPOSE

To encourage children to develop ways of singing well.

RESOURCES

Any song. Here are a few ideas to start you off:

'I went to the Animal Fair'

'Row, row, row your boat'

'Bob the builder'

'One man went to mow'

'She'll be coming round the mountain'

'Five little speckled frogs'

'Pease pudding hot'

'Oh my Darlin' Clementine'

'If you're happy and you know it'

You can find more ideas for songs and melody lines at the Kickstart Music section of www.acblack.com/music

1. The children need to know the chosen song well before refining the way they sing it. Make sure they are very comfortable with the words. When you teach a new song, teach the melody and the words by rote/by ear: you sing a line, they sing it back. Sing through the first verse together.

2. Discuss the words and talk them through before you sing the song again. Try whispering the words together – it encourages children to articulate clearly and improves their diction.

3. Try lots of different ways to sing each verse.
   Sing it:
   - Very loudly (but not shouting).
   - With eyes closed.
   - To la/oo/ah/ee/pa.
   - Alternate lines by alternate groups of children.
   - Happily.
   - Sadly.
   - With actions.
   - For dancing or to create a theatrical effect.

   Ask some children to listen and comment on the 'performance'.

REMEMBER

Standing or sitting up on chairs is much preferable to sitting on the floor when singing. Children can breathe more freely if their chests are not constricted.

Children will always copy the model provided by the teacher. If you sing shyly and quietly, they will sing back diffidently. If you sing confidently and with energy they will reply the same way.

Not all children will be physically able to sing in tune at this stage – do not stop them trying and they will gradually gain more control of their voice

4. Sing unaccompanied almost all the time. Singing entirely unaccompanied helps children to hear more accurately what they are singing than if they are accompanied by percussion or a piano.

5. Starting and stopping together are important. Use visual and musical signals rather than spoken signals where possible. Make sure there is silence before you start and after you finish to give a frame round the song.

6. It's best to make sure everyone knows the first note you have chosen to start on. Sing (on the opening note): "Here's your note – shall we start…" If you just launch in, the children will find your pitch, but make sure you sing high enough for them. Sometimes children growl, not because they can't hear the note, but because the pitch of the song is set too low for them to physically find the note.

Climbing caterpillar

1. Use the natural speech rhythms of the poem below. Start at the bottom of the rhyme below and read upwards (first line is 'Caterpillar slowly crawls').

2. Play the corresponding chime bar at the beginning of each line.

3. All start the song in crouch position gradually getting taller as the tune rises. Drop back down to a crouch on "DROP!". Demonstrate first before singing and doing the actions together. Start at the bottom with the caterpillar crawling up the flower stalk.

C – She will never,   DROP!

B – Won't give up until she's there,

A – Reaching for the top,

G – Stretches further up the stalk,

F – Reaches for the flower,

E – Stretches up then curves her back,

D – Up the flower stalk

C – Caterpillar slowly crawls,

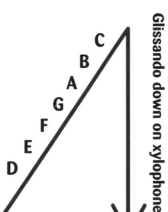

(Glissando down if using a xylophone. Put the beater onto the highest note (C) and run it downwards until you reach the lower C - see diagram).

PURPOSE
To encourage children to respond to music with body movement.

RESOURCES
Chime bars or xylophone up-ended

C,D,E,F,G,A,B,C

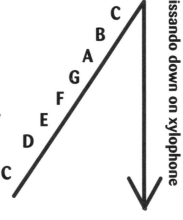

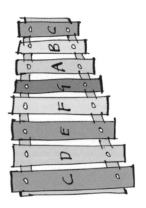

Sounds and Invention

This section includes activities which will encourage children to discover and develop their own library of musical sounds, ways to combine those sounds to make musical patterns and sequences, and ways to improvise musical ideas. They will be given opportunities to invent their own music, refine it and perform it to others.

What does it sound like?

1. Children close their eyes and everyone is very still.

2. Everyone listens for about a minute in silence for any sounds at all that they can hear inside and outside the classroom.

3. In pairs, one child tries to imitate vocally one of the sounds they have heard and the other tries to guess what it was, and vice versa.

4. When they have imitated several sounds, the whole class shares the sounds they found, in groups. For example: all the 'cars revving up' sounds demonstrate their imitation together; all the 'doors slamming' sounds demonstrate their imitation together, and so on.

5. Play a repeated note quickly on a xylophone. Everyone repeats their sounds in groups in an agreed order over the xylophone note, trying to make it into a steady rhythm. You will find that a steady repeated note (called an **ostinato**) will be enough to bind the sounds together into an embryonic piece of music.

6. Everyone closes their eyes again and listens to see if the sounds are different or have changed.

VARIANT

1. Try a similar activity linked to opportunities beyond the classroom, eg, a nature walk.

PURPOSE

To encourage children to recognise sounds that can be used to make music.

REMEMBER

This very simple exercise can be used as a warm up to main musical sessions.

You can use the **ostinato** idea to bind lots of disparate ideas together into a satisfactory whole.

Sound box

1. Listen to each object from the sound box in turn. Discuss the sounds it can make and ways to make these sounds (by tapping, scraping, shaking).

2. Allow the children to have free play/exploration with the soundmakers, both individually and in groups.

3. Put sounds together in a sequence. Encourage children to invent their own sequences.

4. Try playing a sequence, then asking another child to reproduce the same sequence.

EXTENSION

1. Draw pictures of sound objects on cards, eg:

Arrange them in patterns and play the sequences produced.

2. Make symbols for the sounds on cards (see below).

Arrange them in patterns and play the sequences again and again until they make a regular rhythm that you could use to accompany a song

 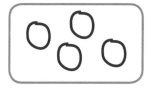

REMEMBER

Value children's ideas for the contents of the box and for the way they use them. Change the contents regularly using a wide variety of objects.

PURPOSE
To encourage the exploration of sound from a variety of sources.

RESOURCES
Keep a brightly coloured 'sound box' in the classroom, containing about six objects at a time. Change contents regularly. They may include corrugated cardboard, an eggbox, a comb, a couple of spoons – anything which makes a sound. Yoghurt pots or pop bottles with different fillings make different sounds, eg, with flour – very soft; with sugar – louder; with lentils – loud. (See more information on www.acblack.com/music.)

How many sounds?

1. Children sit in a circle.

2. Teacher chooses an instrument/soundmaker, eg, a long tube (called a 'boomwhacker').

3. The chosen instrument/soundmaker is passed round the circle in time to the words:

   Magic form, magic form
   How many sounds can you make?

4. At the word "make," the child holding the soundmaker finds a way of making a sound with it, eg, whirls it round his head, blows down it, taps it, rubs it.

5. Continue the game until someone repeats a sound, then change the instrument.

EXTENSION

1. Try making unconventional sounds with conventional instruments, eg, rolling a ping pong ball on a xylophone.

2. Collect four unusual sounds the class has found and arrange them in an interesting sequence with sounds repeated lots of times. Talk about how to improve your 'piece of music'.

PURPOSE

To encourage children to explore the potential for a variety of sounds from a single sound source.

RESOURCES

A variety of instruments and soundmakers (see page 54 resources box).

Conversations

1. Discuss the nature of a verbal conversation.
   For example, first one person says something, then another.
   Occasionally they both talk at the same time or pause before
   they answer; sometimes they talk very quickly, laugh in the
   middle, or shout.

2. Two children sit face to face with instrument(s) between them.

3. They have a musical 'conversation', as in section 1, above. First
   one person plays a short rhythm or tune on their instrument or
   soundmaker, then another responds. Their response could be
   longer or shorter, louder or softer, slower or quicker, or both
   people might play together.

4. Explore ways of varying the mood and development of the
   dialogue: have an argument, or one player echoes the other.
   Each player could take on a character, eg, one slow and gentle,
   the other fast and loudly argumentative.

5. Finishing can be a problem. If so, discuss with the children
   what clues might be used to bring the conversation to an end.
   It's good sometimes to have a third person listening to the
   conversation and then saying if they enjoyed the music or not,
   and why.

PURPOSE
To develop
improvisation skills
and playing control.

RESOURCES
One or two
percussion
instruments. If using
pitched percussion,
make sure each child
has a pair of beaters.

REMEMBER
This works well if
the children play
independently in
a 'music area' with
instruments.

Young children often
find sharing ideas and
co-operating difficult.
Working in pairs
provides them with
a certain amount of
control.

Writing sounds down

1. Children have one instrument between two.

2. They find two or three sounds they like.

3. Ideas are then shared with the whole class.

4. A child plays an idea – the whole class decides on a symbol to represent it. For example:

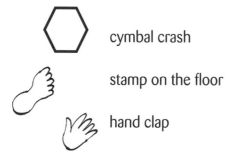

cymbal crash

stamp on the floor

hand clap

5. Make a pattern of the symbols on paper, eg:

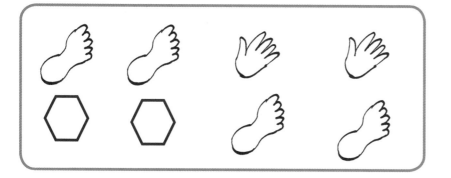

'Play' the pattern several times, keeping the rhythm going.

6. Children make their own patterns for others to 'play'. Arrange sounds in an order – decide on symbol for each sound. Potato or lino prints are excellent for this exercise.

PURPOSE

To encourage children to find ways of recording the sounds and musical ideas they make up.

RESOURCES

A variety of instruments.

Paper and crayons.

REMEMBER

Repetition of ideas is very common in making music. Patterns like this are an excellent introduction to score writing/recording.

Using Stories

1. Children sit in a circle.

2. Read a story, stopping to identify the places for sounds. The example here is 'The Gruffalo' a well-known children's story by Julia Donaldson, but it is possible to use other descriptive stories or to try more than one over time. This story describes various animals that meet the mouse (a fox, an owl, a snake and the Gruffalo). Find sounds to represent them all.

3. Decide on the sounds to use and prepare the children to use them.

4. Read the story pausing for the sounds of the animals eg, guiro rhythm for the snake, eerie bark for the fox and vocal hooting for the owl.

5. Develop a range of voices for the characters and intersperse with the animal sounds.

VARIANT

Use other stories, eg:
- 'The Haunted House'
- 'The Ghost'
- 'Little Red Riding-Hood'
- 'Goodnight owl'
- 'Peace at last'

EXTENSION

Link a story to a song or music to listen to, eg:
- Story – 'The Ghost'
- Song – 'Halloween's Coming'
- Music – 'Danse Macabre' by Saint-Saëns'

PURPOSE

To encourage children to experiment with sound using a story stimulus.

RESOURCES

A variety of instruments and soundmakers.

Descriptive stories for example 'The Gruffalo' by Julia Donaldson.

REMEMBER

Discussion about the choice of sounds to represent elements in the story is very important. Take time over the process of selection.

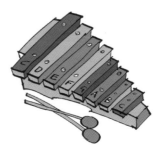

Simple scores

1. Groups of children choose three or four cards and order them in any way they wish, eg:

2. Once they have decided on their sequence, the children should practise playing it.

3. Provide an opportunity for each group to perform to the other children.

EXTENSION

1. Arrange more cards for a longer piece.

2. The children rearrange the cards and invent their own sequence. Repetition can make a piece more interesting,

3. Arrange cards in two rows so that two instruments play at once.

PURPOSE
To invent and write down short sequences of sounds.

RESOURCES

A selection of percussion instruments and corresponding pictures.

Soundscape

1. Children sit or stand in a circle.

2. Show the picture. Discuss with the children what is happening – identify areas where sound could be used to illustrate it.

3. Explore how these sounds could be made. Use body sounds, voices, conventional instruments, junk instruments and objects in the room.

4. Decide what order the sounds should come in.

5. Gradually build up a soundscape to illustrate the picture – 'make the picture talk'.

EXTENSION

1 The class can, together, make a 'plan' or 'score' of their piece and display it next to the picture, or produce a recording of the piece.

2. Limit the time available for the soundscape or it can drag terribly. Try a sandtimer or stopwatch. Give the children several short sessions of no more than 5 minutes, rather than one long one.

PURPOSE
To encourage children to experiment with sound in response to a picture stimulus.

RESOURCES

A descriptive picture, with plenty of possibilities for sound, eg, a page of book, or a big display the children have made in the school hall.

A variety of instruments/sound sources as chosen by the children.

Paper, crayons and a recording device for the Extension.

REMEMBER

At this stage, most of the focus will be on 'sound effects' rather than music or the more abstract qualities of the picture. The use of an ostinato as in 'What does it sounds like?' page 53, would help to bind it together musically.

Sound pictures

1. Children lay all their sound-making objects onto a large piece of card to create a picture. Play all the soundmakers to be sure of what they sound like.

2. Decide on an order of sounds. Which order will you make the sounds on your picture? ie. by hitting, scraping, pulling and so on. Play all or some of the soundmakers in the picture in your preferred order.

3. When children are happy with the order of sounds, they can draw them on a piece of paper. Each sound requires a picture/symbol, eg:

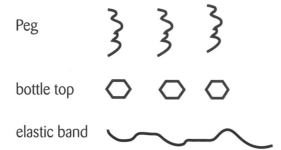

Peg

bottle top

elastic band

PURPOSE
To take early steps towards a child's own composition by providing an opportunity to explore more sound sources and arrange ideas in sequences.

RESOURCES

A variety of sound sources, eg, tissue paper, bottle tops, elastic bands, combs, pegs, card, shells, corrugated card.

4. Their musical picture could look like this:

5. Play it several times (at least three or four) without stopping.

6. Make an audio recording of the piece of music and follow the picture of the music as it is played back. You can also put images onto a computer, assign an instrument for each picture and play as you watch the display on the interactive whiteboard or screen.

VARIANT

1. Produce a picture that can be 'played' by someone else.

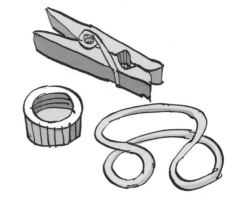

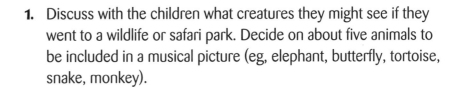
Safari

PURPOSE

To encourage exploration and invention within a given structure and produce an extended piece of music.

RESOURCES

Large picture showing a 'plan' of the music, in this case a visit to a Safari Park. You may develop this as the activity progresses, or have it prepared beforehand.

Alternatively, use video footage of animals.

Selection of sound sources.

1. Discuss with the children what creatures they might see if they went to a wildlife or safari park. Decide on about five animals to be included in a musical picture (eg, elephant, butterfly, tortoise, snake, monkey).

   If you are using video footage, tell the children the animals you have on it for your musical pictures.

2. With two or three children, make a musical picture of another animal (eg, a mouse), as a model. It might include sounds like this:
   - Running up, down and around very quickly, all over a xylophone.
   - Squeaking noises with vocal sounds, a scraper and/or Indian bells.

   When the sounds are all decided, play a repeated note on the chime bar and then play the whole piece together.

3. When you are confident the children know what to do, divide them into six groups: elephants, butterflies, tortoises, snakes, monkeys (or the animals you have on your video footage), and a car group, to make the journey through the safari park.

4. Discuss suitable sounds/music for each animal, eg:
   - Butterfly – fast, quiet, repetitive, high and light.
   - Elephant – loud, slow, heavy and low.

5. Each group chooses instruments and works out its own section of the music.

6. Listen to everyone's music. Discuss it with the class, eg, "Is the elephant music slow enough?" Give the children more time to refine and practise their sequences. This process may take several sessions.

REMEMBER

This activity is intended to last over several sessions. It would be very difficult to complete in one session. It lends itself well to children working on the sections on their own between music sessions, maybe in a music area. It is also very suitable for a long cross-curricular activity.

7. Whole class performance
- Use your finger or a pointer/stick to follow the car trail along the line from start to exit.
- The car group plays at the beginning and between every section.
- When your finger enters the elephant area, the car stops and the elephant music starts.
- When it leaves, the music stops and the car music starts up again – and so on.
- When you reach the Exit, everyone shouts "Goodbye!" (Or, of course, play the video and the appropriate music is played with each animal.)

8. Discuss the performance. How can it be improved? Did everyone come in at the right time? Did anyone forget to play? Were there any gaps between sections? Should you play it again?

VARIANT

1. Make each musical animal picture as a whole class activity over several sessions and then play as a continuous single piece at the end.

2. Vary the details on the plan or the video footage – you could try depicting a walk in space or a visit to the circus.

3. Video the whole performance to play back and discuss.

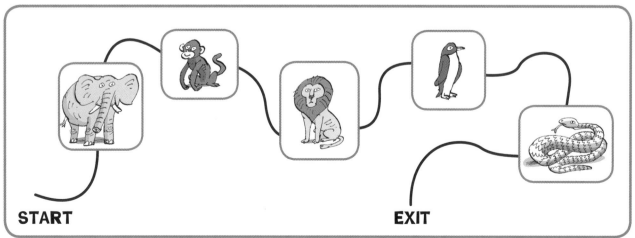

START   **EXIT**

Resources

EQUIPMENT

Many of the activities in the book can be done without any instruments or soundmakers, or with simple soundmakers (such as home-made or found objects), but it is always desirable to build a collection of good quality and easily accessible instruments. **Pitched instruments** might include xylophones, glockenspiels, chime bars and ocarinas, as well as piano, keyboards and other instruments children are learning in school, such as steel pans, trumpets or violins.
Unpitched percussion instruments might include various sized drums and tablas, cymbals, bells and other resonant instruments, tambourines, rattles and other shakers, guiros and other scrapers. **Good quality beaters** are very important in getting the best quality sound from these instruments.

SONGS AND ACTIVITIES

No list could ever be comprehensive in an area such as this. There are many more songbooks as well as those listed here and teachers will have a fund of their own songs whilst being unaware of the origins. Some examples include 'Okki-Tokki-Unga', 'Three Singing Pigs', 'Three Rapping Pigs', 'Banana Splits', 'Sonsense Nongs', 'Bobby Shaftoe, Clap your Hands', 'Someone's Singing, Lord' and 'Tam Tam Tambalay'. For details and a full song index visit the Kickstart Music section of www.acblack.com/music.

RECORDED MUSIC

This list is in no way exhaustive or prescriptive and there are many more ideas on the website. It is merely a list of music used successfully by many teachers for activities like these. There has been no attempt to include suggestions for modern popular music in this list, not as a result of any value judgement, but because fashion and availability is continually changing:

- **Albinoni** Adagio
- **Benjamin** Jamaican Rumba
- **Berlioz** Symphonie Fantastique
- **Brubeck** Unsquare Dance
- **Copland** Fanfare for the Common Man
- **Debussy** La Mer
- **Dukas** The Sorcerer's Apprentice
- **Glass (Philip)** Glassworks
- **Grieg** Peer Gynt Suite
- **Holst** The Planets Suite
- **McCartney** Yesterday and other songs
- **Mendelssohn** The Hebrides Overture
- **Miller/Gordon/Warren** Chattanooga Choo Choo
- **Prokofiev** Peter and the Wolf
- **Saint-Saëns** Carnival of the Animals
- **Saint-Saëns** Danse Macabre
- **Tchaikovsky** The Nutcracker Suite
- **Vaughan Williams** Fantasia on Greensleeves
- **Stravinsky** Petrushka
- **Vivaldi** Four Seasons
- **Waldenfeld** Skaters Waltz

FOR MORE INFORMATION ON RESOURCES AND A FULL SONG LIST VISIT THE KICKSTART MUSIC SECTION OF WWW.ACBLACK.COM/MUSIC